Praise for YE Hui

"Ye Hui's poems in *The Ruins* feel like mathematical equations that never quite add up. They seem eminently logical, yet they defy logic, as in 'The Prophecy' where 'In the yard, two birds perch in the tree/Which means it will snow tomorrow.' These poems are grounded in nature—mountains, birds, fireflies, yet they stay alight, sometimes an inch off the ground; other times, circulating in the metaphysical world. In their collage imagery, these beautiful and pensive poems seem to ask questions of everything—the day about grief, the night about light, this world about the next."

—Victoria Chang, author of *OBIT*

"These are poems that create their own unostentatious universe, inviting us in with subtle gestures that seem to know our own minds better than we do. Once inside, we gradually come to understand this world to be our own, recognizable yet cast in a new light by Ye Hui's acute vision and imaginative power. Here, tradition and universals are pitted against the contemporary condition, not in competition but in fruitful tension, a kind of metaphysical dance. Dong Li, himself a masterful poet, renders these verses with precision and verve, a testament to what translation can accomplish when practiced at its highest level. Here, in the space opened up to us, "there aren't unicorns or swords / But the void when the truth comes into view."

—Eleanor Goodman, translator and author of *Nine Dragon Island*

"Ye Hui has accomplished true independence, something increasingly rare in contemporary poetry. He is not associated with any group or tendency, and his poems are unlike anyone else's. In his work, he transports us to places that are familiar, but seen for what they are—the invisible ripples of an indifferent universe. He writes: 'The fireflies, now bright, now dim / Just as we live but use up all the wisdom / That lights up what's behind us.' He recognizes we are isolated from each other and the world is inexplicable: 'Besides, how can you explain / The hand that once waved you farewell / Now holds in some courtyard / A pot with a long handle burning.' Inhabitants of a broken world, and knowing our shared fate, Ye Hui never loses his tender feelings for his subjects: 'We walk into a house / Cooling from many who have died there.' These are poems we need."

—**John Yau, author of** ***Diary of Small Discontents: New & Selected Poems 1974–2024***

"While it may be true, as poet-translator Dong Li explains, that Ye Hui 'does not belong to any school, clique, or scene,' of contemporary Chinese poetry, the poems in *The Ruins* display a deeper, timeless kinship that transcends language, style, and even culture. Dong Li's renditions into English allow the reader to glimpse the abiding mystery lurking just beneath the surface of Ye's poems. Rereading them over several months, as they now routinely beckon my return, I have come to recognize an underlying wisdom I now identify as uniquely Ye's. We are so lucky to have these strange and magnificent poems in English, to incite our wonder as we face 'the void when the truth comes into view.'"

—**Shook, poet, translator, and founder of Phoneme Media**

遗址

THE RUINS

叶辉 著

YE Hui

Translated from the Chinese
by Dong LI 李栋 译

DEEP VELLUM PUBLISHING
DALLAS, TEXAS

Deep Vellum Publishing
3000 Commerce St., Dallas,Texas 75226
deepvellum.org · @deepvellum

Deep Vellum is a 501c3 nonprofit literary arts organization founded in 2013 with the mission to bring the world into conversation through literature.

Originally published in Mandarin Chinese as 《遗址》 by EP Books Shanghai/ Changjiang Literature & Art Publishing House, Wuhan, P.R. China, 2019

First English edition, 2025

Support for this publication has been provided in part by grants from the National Endowment for the Arts, the Texas Commission on the Arts, the City of Dallas Office of Arts and Culture, and the Addy Foundation.

ISBNs: 978-1-64605-405-3(paperback) | 978-1-64605-406-0 (ebook)

LCCN 2025027171

Cover art and design by Lexi Earle
Interior layout and typesetting by KGT

PRINTED IN THE UNITED STATES OF AMERICA

目录 / CONTENTS

遗址

THE RUINS

Translator's Note

Dong Li

The Chinese poet Ye Hui does not belong to any school, clique, or scene, nor does he teach writing or organize literary festivals. Entirely independent, he occupies a liminal space where the poet Fernando Pessoa meets the painter Agnes Martin. Ye Hui lives in the same countryside where he was born and raised, and his writing keeps growing from the same rain and clouds. He has built his own house—a communal space for his neighbors and passing strangers—and a museum for his village. He collects old and discarded stuff, preserves examples of the local bricks and woods, and keeps the ancient Yangtze Delta culture and landscape from fading into oblivion. It would be easy to compare him to Fernando Pessoa as Ye Hui clerks in a taxation bureau, daydreaming of the contemporaneousness of all ages and countries. Unlike Pessoa, his alter egos exist in the real world. An architect bred of poetry, he builds houses in the countryside that draw in large city crowds and inspire young people's interest in coming back to serve the land, instead of climbing the capitalistic ladders in overpopulated and polluted megacities; as a taxation specialist, he understands the numbers and how to make these architectural visions financially viable and user friendly to people from all backgrounds. Unlike Agnes Martin, he does not shun the public eye but continues to sit out his free hours in a tiny office room, "rioting through the wild," and takes his time in putting out a book of poetry every ten years, each an event. Awarded numerous prizes in recent years, he has a following that is committed and increases with time. He complains he cannot go on writing but moves forward to absorb every influence, foreign or local, from a young writer in obscurity to a little wildflower on his porch in the glory of the morning dew. Everything goes into his poems, into his commitment to a life breathing poetry.

Perhaps the only metaphysical poet among contemporary Chinese poets, as well as the only intimate knower of the *I-Ching*, Ye Hui weaves Chinese metaphysics into real-life snapshots and creates compelling collages of myths and mysteries. A local candy shop becomes a "warm flow" of seething imagination. The terror of "our two hands" on the butcher's table shifts to a mirror image of the self "[u]nfurling by the window" as snow falls. Anything can happen and happens in a Ye Hui poem. Even deadwood can point out "every direction." His poetry "falls like showers," the tug and release of energy that gives everything a new rinse and shine. No wonder he named his house "the villa of showers." However, these showers of myths and mysteries are not meant to mystify and confuse, instead, they are often prophetic, "For a moment, pandemics and slaughters," or metaphorical, "The fireflies, now bright, now dim / Just as we live but use up all the wisdom / That lights up what's behind us," or bracingly upfront, "A house mustn't be built in a land of scorpions and snakes." In his poems, the natural world and the human sphere blend into each other, but they do not turn into surreal kitsch. In an egalitarian fashion, "intellectually disabled kids" are "incarcerated angels," and passengers stuck at a train station overnight become "saints." His restrained poems predate the recent rise of ecopoetics in China and resemble closely the classical Chinese awareness of our ecosphere while remaining entirely readable and contemporary.

Not trying to impress with grand philosophical arguments or linguistic gymnastics, Ye Hui's quiet poems draw us in, slowly, and make us see how his mind drifts into new realities. In the poem "The Prophecy," "two birds perch in the tree," predicting first snow and then death that comes with an unknown flower and its "blinding blue." In a hotel "[t]hat was converted from an old building," a dispirited face appears in "a fog and a fine scent," and as a terrifying past is about to be unveiled, everything is again obscured among "[t]he world of grasses and trees." On a highspeed train, death is both humiliation and humility, revealing its "inborn wildness." Rather than fleshing out his thoughts, Ye Hui's poems make us think and stretch our minds into unseen territories. Not unlike the classical

Chinese masters, whose brushstrokes leap from one image to another, Ye Hui's thoughts spring from one context to another in concentric circles, orbiting a poetic quest for the contemporaneousness of all things. Is Ye Hui a metaphysical poet who restrains himself from abstraction? Is he a meditative poet whose multifaceted realities merge into a dizzying radiance? Is he a transcendental poet who dismantles boundaries in a shift of thought? He seems to be all these things. Rarely do poetry and philosophy converge, but they do in Ye Hui's questing poetics that reaches for the common source and the little freedoms that reside in our restless minds, overcoming "the cold and the night." Despite the metaphysical tensions in his poems, their titles are mostly concrete nouns ("The House," "The Moon," "The Fallacy," "The Waiting Room," etc.), fully anchored in the real, as the naming of things creates worlds and bonds us. Inside his poems, we find ourselves in a strange place, strangely called the planet Earth, our home. This is an ancient Chinese sensibility, where things become more than themselves through poetic association and strike out new spaces for changes in the real world.

Ye Hui has never penned a political statement, nor does he have such ambitions, but a political reading of his poems is as tangible as it is prescient. Quiet resistance unfolds in the poetic ambiguities and extends beyond the poems. Ye Hui is not exiled abroad, nor does he write in a foreign language, but he seems to know all the languages of the heart. Here we have a witch poet of the metaphysical kind that walks backward into the future, an architect of poetic spaces that dispel illusions and invite us into communal living, a poetry that comes from an ancient wisdom that takes a stand against the quarrels of the marketplace and the terror of capitalism, one that keeps company under a leaky authoritarian roof and rubs off its burn, carving out its own freedom, a seeming impossibility in an impossible land. Ye Hui is a discovery and an exemplar of contemporary Chinese poetry, and at its best, his is a poetry full of revelations. After reading Ye Hui's poems, you don't know where you are, and you feel, for a moment, as if you were Chinese.

第一辑

Part I

一首中国人关于命运的诗

我用别针钉死一只蜘蛛
那却不是我的缘故

一个妓女对警察说
我也不想干，但没办法

其实这是一种古老的说法，无论我在哪里
总是同一个地方

一个工人从脚架手架上摔下来
也是几十年注定的

尽管那时还没有这座建筑，没有
建造它的蓝图，甚至想要建造它的人还未出生

我向西会影响他人，向南则损害自己

而我女儿几个世纪前就已出生
她如此苍老，我又如此年轻

被伤害的人又回到伤害他的人身边
像只来回镖，在它的弧形空间里

有一回，我看到了黄河
一条泛滥的生命线，我却弄不清
它是否与我有关

A Poem on the Chinese Perspective on Fate

I use a pin to crucify a spider
But that's not for my own sake

A prostitute says to a policeman
I don't want to do this but have no other way

In fact, there's an old saying: wherever I am
It is always the same place

A worker falls from the scaffolding
That was fated decades ago

Though there was no such building then, nor blueprint
Even those who wanted to build it were not yet born

To the west I bother others, to the south I hurt myself

My daughter was born many centuries ago
She's so old, and I'm so young

Those who were hurt go back to those who hurt them
Like a return dart tracing its own arc

Once I saw the Yellow River
A flooded lifeline, but I cannot figure out
Whether it has anything to do with me

在糖果店

有一回我在糖果店的柜台上
写下一行诗，但是
我不是在写糖果店
也不是写那个称秤的妇人
我想着其他的事情：一匹马或一个人
在陌生的地方，展开
全部生活的戏剧，告别 、相聚
一个泪水和信件的国度
我躺在想像的暖流中
不想成为我看到的每个人
如同一座小山上长着
本该长在荒凉庭院里的杂草

At the Candy Shop

Once on the counter of the candy shop
I wrote down a line of poetry, but I
Didn't write about the candy shop
Or the lady who weighed the goodies, I was
Thinking about other stuff: a horse or a person
Unfolding in a strange place
All the theatres of life: partings, gatherings
A land of letters and tears
I lay in the warm flow of the imagination
And didn't want to become everyone I'd seen
Like the weeds on a hill that should have grown
In a desolate courtyard rioting through the wild

在乡村

在乡村，我们开始谈论命运
我们在一张屠桌上
铺上白桌布，它就变成一张会议桌
那样我们可以安心地
把两只手放上去

在其它情形里，有人说：床已经铺好了
但我不知道说话的是谁
是怎样的一只手
还有油灯边那张年轻姑娘的脸
悲哀，还是羞怯
以及户外是哪个时代的迷雾

漫延开来，在我站着的窗前
像在一面镜子前
白雪落到了镜中

In the Countryside

In the countryside, we start to talk about fate
On a butcher's table, we spread a white cloth
To turn it into a conference table
Thus, we can peaceably
Put our two hands on it

In another situation, someone says: the bed's been made
But I don't know who's talking
What kind of a hand it was
Or the young woman's face by the oil lamp
Sadness or is it shyness
Or a fog from an unknown era outside

Unfurling by the window
Where I stand as if before a mirror
Into which clean snow falls

萤火虫

在暗中的机舱内
我睁着眼，城市的灯火之间
湖水正一次次试探着堤岸

从居住的小岛上
他们抬起头，看着飞机闪烁的尾灯
没有抱怨，因为

每天、每个世纪
他们经受的离别，会像阵雨一样落下

有人打开顶灯，独自进食
一颗星突然有所觉悟，飞速跑向天际

这些都有所喻示，因此
萤火虫在四周飞舞，像他们播撒的
停留在空中的种子

萤火虫，总是这样忽明忽暗
正像我们活着
却用尽了照亮身后的智慧

The Fireflies

In the darkness of the cabin
My eyes are open: between city lights
The lake probes and probes the shore

From their habitat on the island
They look up at the plane's flickering taillights
And have no complaints, since

Every day, every century
The separation they endure falls like showers

Someone turns on the overhead light and eats alone
A star has a sudden epiphany and races to the horizon

All these are metaphors, thus
The fireflies dance around, like the seeds they sow
That remain in the air

The fireflies, now bright, now dim
Just as we live but use up all the wisdom
That lights up what's behind us

预言

两只鸟歇在
院中的树上，表明天要下雪了
火在炉膛里，树叶
还在飘落。有人在敲门，还有
另外一些声音
傍晚时，我已经能听得很远，几十里之内
没有人在哭泣，霜在
山谷中凝成。木头房子里
有人将死去，在一块被温暖过的
石头旁，一个女人
采下了一朵我们没有见过的花
那不能正视的比寒冷和夜晚
更深的蓝

The Prophecy

In the yard, two birds perch in the tree
Which means it will snow tomorrow
Fire in the stove, leaves still fall
Someone knocks on the door
And there are other noises
In the evening, I can hear far, miles away
No one cries, the valley frosts
In the wooden house, someone is dying
And by a warmed-up stone
A lady picks a flower
That we've never seen
Its blinding blue, bluer
Than the cold and the night

陌生的小镇

丢失家园的人，远眺群山
尽管那里不是他的家

鹭鸶吃饱后，站在湖边
等待着太阳落下

每一道墙的阴影里
总有人小声地交谈着

一个月前，我父亲去世
房子外面站着一个人，正在等车

那人手里擎着一枝花，旁边蹲着
一条带链子的狗

车来了吗……
看来，我们已经各就各位了

看来，枯树枝
已经指明了所有方向

The Uncanny Town

A person who has lost his homeland looks
Far into the mountains though that's not his home

After eating its fill, a heron stands by the lake
Waiting for the sun to set

In the shadow of every wall
Someone whispers in a low voice

My father died a month ago, outside our house
Stood a person, waiting to be picked up

The person held a flower in his hand, next to him
Squatted a dog on a chain

Is the vehicle here now . . .
It seems we are all in our places

It seems deadwood has already
Pointed out every direction

飞鸟

音乐无所谓

诗歌可读的不多

湖边的清新空气
只对肺有所帮助

一年之中，我很少做梦
有几次冥想

我的生活，离不开其他人

有些人，我不知道姓名
还有些已经死去

他们都在摇曳的树叶后面看我
如果我对了
就会分掉一些他们的幸福

鸟飞过来了

那些善意的鸟，为什么
每次飞过时
我都觉得它们会投下不祥

The High-Flying Birds

Music does not matter

Not much poetry to read

The fresh air by the lake
Only helpful to the lungs

Throughout the year, I rarely dream
But meditate a few times

My life depends on others

Some people, whose names I don't know
Others, already dead

They watch me from behind
The swaying leaves, if I'm right
I take a cut of their happiness

The high-flying birds are here

Those kind birds, why
Do I feel the bad omens they'll drop
Each time they pass

果树发芽、开花的季节

在这条街上，我听到尽头的果园中
风整夜拍打着一扇木门，拍打着
我见过的那扇门，此时树的影子
在其上投下一只只柔软的手，在南方果树
发芽、开花的季节，仿佛一种阴森的祭奠仪式
正在进行，我读着一本书，在今天
在一百年前一个少年成了它愉快的供品
透过树叶我看到比十九世纪
更蓝的天空，另一个少年的灵魂
又要升上去了，有如洗笔水中再滴入
一滴纯蓝墨水，他的到来的芬芳，却比果园还要馥郁
却不知已踏入一种古老的循环之中
在这个甜美的夜里，我庆幸自己不再年少
可是，我突然感到我曾腰缠软剑，袖藏飞刀
感到左手不知道右手要干什么

The Season When Fruit Trees Sprout and Bloom

In the orchard at the end of the street, I hear the wind
Beating all night on the wooden gate, beating
The gate that I've seen, at this moment, tree shadows
Cast many a gentle hand in the southern season
When fruit trees sprout and bloom, as if an eerie ritual
Of sacrifice is taking place, I'm reading a book, today
A hundred years ago, a youngster was its pleasant offering
And through the capillaries, I see a sky more blue
Than the nineteenth century, the soul of another youngster
Arises soon, as if dropping another drop of pure blue ink
In the washing water, his arrival more fragrant than the orchard
Yet not knowing that he has stepped into the ancient circulation
In this sweet evening, I'm happy that I'm no longer young
Then out of the blue, I feel I once had a soft sword around my waist
And flying knives in my sleeves, I feel my left hand not knowing
What my right hand is about to do

联系

扁豆与牵牛花
散发出一阵淡淡的雨水气味

宛如一段关于
未来生活的预言

一只黑嘴鸟停在
谷仓的沉静气息里，而附近
破败寺庙的放生池中
大鱼生出了小鱼

我记得我曾跑向一个庭院
它的石阶上有一束
被扔弃的枯萎的玫瑰

在房里的桌子上
玻璃花瓶里只盛着
半瓶清水

The Connection

Lentils and morning glories
Emit a faint smell of rain

Like a prophecy
On life in the days to come

A black-billed bird settles
In the barn's hushed breath, and nearby
In the release pond of a shabby temple
A big fish breeds a small fish

I remember I ran to a courtyard
On whose cobble steps lay
A discarded, wilted rose

On the table in the room
A glass vase holds water and is only
Half full

参观

我们走进一座房子
它因其中死去过很多人而阴凉

它曾是谷仓、医院
和审讯室

墙上挂着铁勾
木制刑具，长条形的桌子上
如今铺着绒布

藤蔓垂挂在窗口
在骤至的风中像以前这里
某个女人的长发

透过宽大的通向后院的门
一棵樟树
摇摆不定，渐渐变黑变大
说不定正在变成神

光线转暗
再也没有谁说话，我们保持缄默
也许就该如此

终于有人开口了：是否还要走下去
灯光亮了
所有的人都大笑起来

The Visit

We walk into a house
Cooling from many who have died there

It used to be a barn, a hospital
And an interrogation room

On the walls hang iron hooks
Wooden torture instruments, long tables
Now covered in flannel

Tendrils drop through the window
And in a sudden wind resemble
A woman's long hair here once before

Past the wide gate that leads to the backyard
There is a camphor tree
That sways and slowly grows big and black
Perhaps it is turning into a god

The light dims
No one talks anymore, we remain silent
Perhaps that's how it should be

Finally someone speaks up: should we go on
The lights are on now
All of us burst into laughter

脸上带着回到家的表情
并且松开了彼此
刚才还紧攥在一起的手

Our faces put on an expression of home
And we let go of each other's hands
That a moment ago were clasped together

陌生人

1

他坐在窗前
一动不动，树叶落到
头上

背后，镜子里
一个裸体的女孩
绻缩在谢顶的国王身体中

她的盔甲散落在地板上
在一方块
黄昏的光线中

外面，刺槐树
瞬间变成
生铁，马群变成石头

The Stranger

1

He sits before the window
Motionless, leaves falling
On his head

Behind his back, in the mirror
A girl naked
Crouches beneath a bald king

Her armor scatters on the floor
In a square
Of twilight

Outside, an acacia turns
In an instant into raw iron
And horses become stones

2

一条路通向
陷没的国土深处

他记得在那里
与一个路人谈论着
天象、瘟役

以及不祥的鸟
还有猫头鹰，你知道
它来自哪里吗

它来自
古代，一只猫的噩梦

他只听到四周
那踏着枯叶的声音
但看不到他的脸

2

A road leads
To the depth of the fallen kingdom

He remembers there
Talking with a passerby
About heavenly signs, plagues

And ominous birds
As well as an owl, do you know
Where it comes from

It arrives
From antiquity, a cat's nightmare

All he hears around him is the sound
Of stepping on dried leaves, but he cannot
See his face

对应

你照过镜子后
那人从背面离开，觉得一阵头晕目眩
一个和你几乎一样的人
不过命运将你左脸上的胎记
放在他右边
但他不在乎，并且他还有一个
与你相近的名字
只是总与你背道而驰：你坐着时
他正躺下，你走在沙漠中
他却在热带避着雨
只有一次你们会有机会擦肩而过
当中隔着道很高的围墙
像很多人那样，他也渐渐成熟
恋爱，有自己的圈子，结婚
那几天他摆脱
一直缠着他的莫名焦虑
房间里放着从野外
剪来的怒放的百合
有人暗示他，在山谷中它的根茎
还在稀里糊涂地生长
他没细想，也没多心
否则他也不会常摸着自己
扁平的肋骨纳闷
或者虽然活得自在、营养丰富
但总感到疲惫软弱
他并不知道，那是因为
他像一棵树，除了枝叶，还有根须

The Correspondence

After you look in the mirror
The person in it leaves from behind, feeling dizzy
Someone almost identical to you
Yet fate puts the birthmark on your left cheek
And on his right
But he doesn't care, and he does have
A name like yours
Yet always opposites: when you sit
He lies down, when you walk in the desert
He takes shelter from the tropical rain
Only once do you have the chance to pass each other
Separated by a high wall
Like others, he matures slowly
Falls in love, forms his circle, and gets married
For a few days, he frees himself
From the inexplicable anxiety that haunts him
In the room blooms a tulip
Picked from the wild
Someone hints at its root in the valley
Which still unknowingly grows
He doesn't think any further, nor does he care too much
Otherwise, he wouldn't touch
His flat ribs and wonder
How he always feels worn out
Though carefree and well-nourished
He doesn't know that's because
He's like a tree, except for the branches and tendrils

有两头的努力，两头的生长
因此，他求助神灵
要么夜观天象，而他却错过了
超验的时机，他祷告
并且下跪，在地上留下两个小坑
晚上地平线上便隆起
两个肌瘤
但这并不影响他活得耐久
我们知道，通常情形下
如保管得当，物质比人长寿
镜子也不例外
即使原形消亡了，它还能再活一段
不然你如何解释
那些死去的人的音容
为何仍会留在活人的记忆中
但有时一个调皮的小孩
在上面的一阵磨擦，让他关节疼痛
或生出一个噩梦
而斑落的镜面，使他的头发
变灰，腹腔上留下
三个小洞。他躺在医院的床上
睁开眼，从而看到
白色的帽子和床单耀眼的光芒
有说不出的感动
感到回到了故乡
感到流下了一滴泪，晶莹、沉重
像水银

He has two ends to work, two ends to grow
Thus, he prays to the gods
To observe the night sky but misses
The timing of transcendence, he prays
And kneels, leaving two small dents on the ground
Leaving two tumors
Rising on the night horizon
But this doesn't keep him from living a long life
We know, under normal circumstances
If well attended to, matter outlives humans
The mirror is no exception
Should its form disintegrate, it can live a bit longer
Otherwise, how can you explain
Why the faces of the dead continue
To live in the memories of the living
But an unruly child sometimes
Rubs on it so that his joints ache
Or he gives birth to a nightmare
The mottled mirror turns his hair gray
And leaves three small holes
In his abdomen as he lies on a hospital bed
Opens his eyes and sees
White hats and the dazzling light of the sheets
Feeling unspeakably moved
As if he has returned home
As if a tear drops, sparkling, heavy
like mercury

面孔

夜晚我看到一张脸
在窗玻璃上，在户外未完成的建筑上
被台灯照亮
仿佛废墟上出现的圣容。在我身后，书架排列在
远处的村落中。一阵黑暗里的犬吠
或者上一场暴雨在地上
留下了持久的光亮
而在这一切的后面，高过群山之上
云团飞舞，急速奔涌
有如多少年来飞逝而去的灵魂

The Face

At night, I see a face
On the windowpane, on the unfinished building outside
Illuminated by the desk lamp
Like a holy countenance above the ruins, behind me
Bookshelves line up in a faraway village, dogs bark
In the dark, and a storm leaves a lasting shine
On the ground, behind all this
Beyond the mountain range
Clouds dance and dart forward
Like all the souls over all these years flying away

一棵葡萄

在街上，一个美丽的妇人
向我抱怨她单调的梦，而我告诉她
应该在她常梦到的地方
植一株葡萄

我说：它将长势旺盛
抽出新芽
并且会很快攀上旁边一棵年老的榆树
要么，缠住一块石头
因此一切会有所不同

要知道，人在这世上
会有另一样东西和他承受
相同的命运

你信不信。你的乳房也将再次充盈
当它长出星小的果实时
一只黑鸟会突如其来地啄食

简直如同闪电
一只黑鸟，来自百里之外一个男人的梦境
并且已被豢养了多年

我不能告诉你他是谁，住在何处
因为一旦说出来，某个院子里
疯长的荒草就会死去

A Grapevine

On the street, a pretty woman complains to me
About her monotonous dreams, and I tell her
To plant a grapevine
At a place she often dreams of

I say: it will grow fast
Put forth new shoots
And soon climb up the old elm next to it
Or it will wrap itself around a rock
Thus, everything will be different

You know, for every person in this world
There is another thing that shares
The same fate with him

Believe it or not, your breast will be full again
When it bears a berry, small like a star
A blackbird will peck at it out of the blue

Quick as lightning, the blackbird appears
From a man's dream hundreds of miles away
And has been bred for years already

I cannot tell you who he is, where he lives
Because if I did, in some courtyard
Wild grasses would die out

关于人的常识

每一个人
总有一条想与他亲近的狗
几个讨厌他的日子
和一根总想绊住他的芒刺

每一个人总有另一个
想成为他的人，总有一间使他
快活的房子
以及一只盒子，做着盛放他的美梦

人行道上的那个广告牌前
站着一个已经死去的人的儿子
他站在父亲以前站立的地方

还有，你如何解释
那只曾向你道了永别的手
如今在某个院子里，正握着
发烫的长柄锅

Common Sense on Being Human

Every person
Has a dog that wants to be close to him
A number of days that loathe him
And a prickle that tries to trip him

Every person has another person
That wants to be him, a house
That makes him happy
And a box that holds his sweet dreams

In front of the billboard on the sidewalk
Stands a dead person's son
He stands where his father once stood

Besides, how can you explain
The hand that once waved you farewell
Now holds in some courtyard
A pot with a long handle burning

第二辑

Part II

远观

从远处，寺院的屋顶
仿佛浮现在古代的暮霭中，钟声似有似无

溪水，仍然有着
修行人清洌的气息

农舍稍稍大了点
土豆仍像尚未穿孔的念珠

这一切都没有改变

除了不久前，灌木丛中，一只鸟翅膀上的血
滴在树叶上，

夜里，仓库中的狗对着自己的
回声吠叫，因为恐惧

一个婴儿死于出生，另一些人在灾难中
获救

大雾看起来像是革命的预言
涌入了城市，当它们散去后

没有独角兽和刀剑
只有真理被揭示后的虚空

The Long View

From afar, the roof of the monastery appears
To emerge in ancient twilight, its bell subdued

The brook continues to breed
The pristine breath of an ascetic

The farmhouse seems a bit too large
The potatoes remain unknotted prayer beads

All this has not changed

Except the blood on a bird's wings in the shrubbery
That not long ago dropped on a leaf

At night, a dog in the barn barks
At its own echo, out of fear

A baby dies at birth, and others in a disaster
Are saved

The fog looks like the prophecy of a revolution
That flows into the city, and after it burns off

There aren't unicorns or swords
But the void when the truth comes into view

月亮

房子的阴影中
站着一个人，猫坐在门洞深处

苔藓、刺槐树
沉浸于古远的静谧

冬夜
中国庭院中，一座空空的凉亭
这些都仿佛获得了永恒

永恒，就是衰老
就是淬火后的，灰暗、冰冷

当夜晚的恐惧
变成了白日的羞愧

三个弱智儿童并排坐在窗下
仰起他们梦幻般的脸

仿佛三个天使
被囚禁在苍白、微弱的光里

The Moon

In the shadow of a house
Stands a man, a cat sits deep in the doorway

Mosses and locust trees
Soak in ancient stillness

A winter night
In a Chinese courtyard, an empty pavilion
These seem to have obtained eternity

Eternity, it is aging
Is the gray and cold after fire's quench

When fear of night
Turns into shame of day

Three intellectually disabled kids sit in a line
Beneath the window, turning up their dream-like faces

As if three incarcerated angels
In the faint, pale light

木偶的比喻

木偶，或许就是
对人的暗示，只是我们看不到
那根线，比蛛丝透明

我照常行走，但有些人
已经倒下，他身后的人走了神
松开了手

父亲躺下几个月后离世
不知什么缘故，院子中的桂花
却开得更盛

几个放风筝的小孩
在对面楼顶嬉闹，天空很蓝
云朵像蚕丝

The Puppet Metaphor

A puppet, perhaps it hints
at a person, but we do not see
The strings, more invisible than the spider's web

I walk as usual, but someone has already
Fallen, the mind behind him blanks
And loosens its grip

After lying down for months, my father died
For no reason, the laurels in the yard
bloomed in full

A few kids that fly kites are playing
On the opposite rooftop, the sky so blue
The clouds a gloss of silk

高速列车

也许是
十九世纪，冬夜的傍晚
乘坐火车去巴黎
裘皮大衣、帽子
小巧的拎包，车厢内
磨得发亮的木板墙
一张脸，从玻璃上返照
那消失的一切

如果我们离开地面
会获得快感

街道湿润
门铃。新近的传闻都在
证实世界的变化
化学品的香气弥漫在
桉树叶间

黑色灵车在天亮前
悄悄运走死者
死是一种羞辱，但有时
是一种卑谦，像旧照片里
窗口的一张张面孔
永远停留在
隐匿的轨道和田野中

The Highspeed Train

It could be a winter
Evening in the nineteenth century
Taking the train to Paris
In a fur coat and hat, holding
A briefcase, in the compartment
Polished wooden walls
And a face, reflected from the glass
All that has vanished

If we float above the ground
There is a sensation

The street wets
The doorbell, recent rumors
Certify worldly changes
The smell of chemicals loose
In the eucalyptus

Before dawn, a black hearse
Quietly carries the dead away, death
A kind of humiliation, yet at times
It is humility, like the faces
By the window in old photos
That stay forever
In hidden tracks and fields

只有一棵孤单的树
在自我制氧

锈蚀的铁轨和
煤烟，仍然要穿过
结合部。拐弯处的弧度
会给沉思带来愉悦
也许我们能及时醒来
并且小跑着下车，或者
继续沉睡，让列车
带着我们穿越薄暮，穿越

终点站。以及之后天生的荒芜
和真正的黑暗

Only a lonesome tree
Oxygenates itself

Soot, rusted tracks
Joints still to be crossed
And the curve of the bend
Brings pleasure to thoughts
Perhaps we will wake in time
And trot off the train or go on
Sleeping and let the train take us
Through the thin dusk, to cross

The end and then the inborn wildness
Then the real absence of light

新闻

我开车、听新闻
离开了城市，田野在路边铺开
野鸡突然笨拙地从
干涸的水渠里飞起，像村上浪荡的少妇
收音机里柔和的语调
灾难、凶杀
和昨天没有区别
河流在远处，如一把剃刀
政治家站上
新材料做成的讲坛时
我经过了
危险的25公里处
在那里，我的几个朋友
曾在深夜的暴雨中，等着救援
流行音乐的间隙中
几名儿童已渡过危险期，但其他地方
火势仍然旺盛
夜幕伴着
亮着灯的窗口到来
没有名字的小集镇，一如继往的生活
旧房子阁楼上的
壁虎关注着蜘蛛网
我，一个平凡生活的爱好者
一个喜欢真实蜂蜜的人
快速冲下山坡，在低谷地带缓慢行驶
一如在思想快乐的晦暗之处

The News

I drive and listen to the news
Now the city drops behind, fields flank the road
In an instant, pheasants fly off clumsily
From dry ditches, like lustful ladies cruising the village
Soft tones on the radio
Disasters and murders
No different than yesterday
The river distant like a razorblade
When politicians stand
On the podium made of new materials
I am past
The dangerous fifteenth mile
Where some of my friends once in a night storm
Waited to be rescued
And in the gaps of pop music
A few kids are out of danger, elsewhere
A fire keeps burning
Night drops its curtain
By the lit windows
On the nameless town, the same life as before
A gecko in the old attic
Watches a spider's web
I, a lover of the quotidian
A connoisseur of real honey
Run quickly down the slope, driving slow in the lowlands
As if in the obscurity of contemplative happiness

声音渐渐变得含混
如同闪电和呼啸汇集的嗡嗡声
像另一种语言，古代或来自中东
这声音让我想起
车灯前曾闪现过的一张脸，在烈火之外的暗处
扎着头巾，或许不是头巾
而是裹在脸上的一块腐烂的布
在夜晚的黑幕前
这张脸，我在哪见到，在什么地方
我按响了喇叭

The noise grows muffled
Like the convergent buzz of lightning and thunder
Like another language from antiquity or the Middle East
This noise reminds me of a face
Flashing before my headlights, in the shadow by the flames
Tied in a turban, perhaps not a turban
But a tattered cloth wrapped around the face
And in front of the night curtain
Is this face, wherever I saw it, anywhere
I beep the horn

上午突然变得喧闹

一群鸟
在对岸飞翔，仿佛在另外的世界

树木，摇晃在自己暗淡的光中
古老的房子正在隐去

只有我明白
其实它们是在不同的时刻、年代里

街道陌生，迎面而来的脸
像一张张树叶
从某个永远看不到的大院中飘来

有人站在深巷中的一道门前
门还未打开

桌前坐着一个男童
从一本摊开的图画本，转过来他苍白的脸
他已死去多年

上午突然变得喧闹

Morning Suddenly Becomes Loud

A flight of birds
Glides on the other bank as if in another world

The trees wave in their own diminished light
The old houses are fading away

Only I know, in fact, they exist
In different ages and moments

On the strange street, faces come my way
Like leaves after leaves that blow
From some courtyard that always lies hidden

Someone stands before a gate in a deep alley
The gate, not yet opened

A boy sits by a desk, a picture book spreads
In front of him, he turns around his ashen face
He has been dead for years

Morning suddenly becomes loud

划船

当我捡起东西时
我看到桌子下面父亲临终的样子
或者向一边侧过身
看到他的脸，在暗处，在阴影中
这阴影是时刻转变
带来的灰烬。因此，我必须有一个合适的姿势
才能静观眼前，犹如在湖上
划船，双臂摆动
夕阳的光像白色的羽毛
慢慢沉入水中，我们又从那里
划到不断到来的记忆中
波浪，展现了它的阴阳两面

Rowing a Boat

When I pick something up
I see my father under the table, dying
Or when I turn to one side
I see his face in the dark, in the shadow
Which is the ash that is brought on
By the changing of times, thus, I must have the right posture
To observe everything before my eyes, as if on the lake
Rowing a boat, arms swinging
And like white feathers, the crepuscular light
Slowly sinks into the water, where we row
Into the oncoming memories and waves
That display the two sides of yin and yang

笑声

要知道，如今做成雕像的人
在更古老的年代可能会制成木乃伊

要知道，不仅仅是灰雀、鹧鸪
在风中还有血液气味，尘土也能飞翔

夜晚一只猫的重瞳反复打量着
有疑问的世界，然后消失在柱石深处

智者不再大笑，他们头上的光环
此刻正变成爆裂前飞溅的思想火花

The Laughter

You know, those who are made into statues today
Could have been mummified in a faraway age

You know, there are not only bullfinches and partridges
But also the smell of blood in the wind, even dust

Can fly, an odd-eyed cat examines and reexamines at night
The doubtful world then disappears into the depth of pillars

They no longer laugh, the wise whose auras now turn
To sparks of thoughts splashing before the blast

夜上海

仿佛被一根缆绳
牵扯着，公共汽车、电梯
木质公寓都在晃动
一个门房在楼梯下的椅子上
瞌睡，摊开的画报上方
电灯昏暗，也许不会再有人回来
在靠近苏州河边
成排的小船已经睡下了
只有仓库边的鬼魂在出没，鸦片的气味
比洋油更浓烈，雪茄
飘散出雪花膏气息，一个喷嚏回荡在
小巷深处，门打开，窗子关闭
调频的声音
依然听上去非常诡秘，在阁楼上
然而夜晚是崭新的，仿佛刚刚擦拭过的
小号，永远指向天花板的深处
暗淡的面颊渐渐明亮
咖啡在杯中散开涟漪
桌子在摇晃，还有床、鞋子、地板上的
一枚锃亮零钱
声音不会死去，它们存放在
胶木唱片那样的地方。而沉默的声音
会消失，一个
陕西商人，拎着沉重的皮箱
走在充满水汽的街道上

Shanghai at Night

As if tethered
By a cable, buses and elevators
And wooden apartments are all shaking
A concierge dozes off in a chair
Downstairs, above the open pictorial
The light bulb dims, perhaps no one will return
On the Suzhou River
Rows of small boats have fallen asleep
Only ghosts appear near the warehouse, the smell
Of opium stronger than imported kerosene, cigars
Emit a scent of cold creams, a sneeze echoes
In the deep alley, doors open, windows close
The frequency modulation still sounds
Intensely obscure, in the attic
The night is yet brand-new, as if a trumpet
Freshly polished, points forever to the deep of the ceiling
Dull cheeks are brightening
Coffee ripples in the cup
The table quivers, so does the bed, shoes
And a shiny coin on the floor
Voices never die, they are kept somewhere
Like vinyl records, but the silent voices
Will vanish, now a merchant from Shaanxi
Carries a heavy leather trunk
And walks on the steamy street

战争已近，上海更远了
像一艘白天还停泊在码头的
外国游轮。在灾难前逃离
它将越来越远
在不死的歌声和海上紫色的闪电中

The war is approaching, Shanghai withdraws
Like a foreign cruise ship moored at the harbor
During the day, an escape before the disaster
Drops further and further into undying
Songs and the purple lightning on the sea

在暗处

树木整夜站在露水中
草地潮湿，或许正在交换它们的种子
而灯光如一道符咒，中止并取消
地下的秘密交易

在可见的边缘
蹲着一只青蛙，正分泌出粘液
人的脸会在玻璃后面出现
身体陷入黑暗，那是未知的
地平线后面，半个世界滚落进海洋

它们终究摆脱了我们，只有
船依然笔直地航行，被暗处的
马达推动着。为什么驱动我们的一切
都来自地下、暗舱和沉重的黑色丝绒

仿佛中世纪女巫的长裙
也许内衬艳如晨曦，在古代希腊或英格兰
石板路上走来一个中国人，也可能
只是长得相像。而如果你有喜悦
身体内就会出现一道闪电

In the Dark

The trees stand all night in the dews
The grasses moist, presumably exchanging their seeds
And like a spell, the light breaks and abolishes
The secret dealings underground

At the visible edge
Squats a frog, secreting its mucus
A human face appears behind the glass
The body sinks into the dark, that unknown beyond
The horizon, where half of the world rolls into the ocean

They are finally rid of us, only a ship
Still sails in a straight line, propelled by the motor
In the shadow, why does everything that drives us always surface
From the subterranean, dark chambers, and heavy black velvets

Like the long dress of a witch in the Middle Ages, its linings
Likely bright like morning light, while in ancient Greece or England
On the cobble street comes someone Chinese, or perhaps
That person just looks Chinese, and if you feel joy
In your body there flares a flash of lightning

异地

只是玻璃、云层
一些细雨，仅有的记忆
挡着我。空气有着
审判的意味。陌生的脸
仿佛是影像，罪犯
自己走向监狱，一个
相反的城市，火车
永远倒走，而且越来越快
漫长的谈判，正在进行
不知为了什么，或者
只是因为气候
细微的失误、漫长的梦
我在各种时差里
所有的人都活着，死
变成某种气质，需要接受治疗
有时，一阵真实的
风吹进来，一小撮花粉
全境戒严
因为失眠，老鼠成了思想家
这里没有夜晚
唯一的奖赏：一张过期多年的车票
或者模拟飞行
稍稍从地面腾空

Elsewhere

Just glass, clouds
Some fine rain, only memories
Hold me back, the air contains
A sense of judgment, strange faces
Resemble images, criminals escort
Themselves into incarceration
An opposite city, a train going forever
Backward and ever faster
A long negotiation is taking place
Not knowing why
Or merely for the weather
The minute negligence, the prolonged dreams
I am in every type of jet lag
All are alive, death turns
Into a certain temperament, needing treatment
Sometimes a real gust of wind blows
Inside, and with a pinch of pollen
The whole land on quarantine
Because of insomnia, a rat becomes a thinker
There is no night here
The meager reward: a ticket expired for years
Or a flight simulator
That quietly lifts off the ground

卷角书

某日，我发现
世界
卷起了一角

像衣领和
书，像烧毁的信

文字也变成灰烬
铅色
飘向永恒

或许写信的人
曾在窗下，背对着我们

煤炉冒着热气
什么人
还没有回到屋中

外面河水的声音
响了一夜，仿佛一个女人
在洗床单

有多少屈辱和污秽
河水清澈
在夜色中如墨

The Dog-Eared Book

One day, I find
The world
Dog-eared

Like a collar or
A book, like a burnt letter

Words turn into ashes
The color of lead drifts
To eternity

Perhaps the letter writer had his
Back to us by the window

The coal stove smokes
Someone is
Not yet home

There's a river outside
Sloshing all night, as if a lady
Now washes her sheets

How much humiliation or filth
The river clear
Running in the night, like ink

灵魂

灵魂爬行。有人告诉我
比成烟雾是历史错误，有些理论认为
它会飞，像枝头鸟，尤其是
黑色的那种，一些文献中有过记载
可能，如同走失的狗，不是认不出你
只是遗传健忘症。它们也会突然亢奋
在月圆夜。而某些时代无精打采
只是跟随人的影子，垂着头

The Soul

The soul crawls, I have been told that it is
A historical mistake to compare it to smoke, some theories say
It can fly, like a bird on a branch, especially
The black kind, which has been documented
Perhaps it is like a lost dog, it's not that it doesn't recognize you
But it suffers from genetic amnesia and becomes suddenly aroused
On a full-moon night, and in certain ages, it is not active
But follows human shadows, its head hanging

礼物

去年，我种丝瓜
长出了几只葫芦

之间很长的日子
平淡。没有任何征兆

我没有看过大海和帆船
我错过了什么

The Gift

Last year, I planted loofahs
And a few gourds grew

The long days in between remained
Uneventful, void of any signs

I haven't seen the sea or a sailboat
What did I miss

在寺院

庙宇，古老的阴影下
坐着一个默不作声的僧侣

祈祷声隐约如远雷
小小的罪过，如雨水在山谷中聚集

一排麻雀站立在屋檐上
像一个个等待超渡的灵魂

而阳光射进大殿
尘埃瞬间凝成的巨大柱梁

傍晚，我终于看到了银杏那浓密的树冠
在一朵欲雨的云下

In the Monastery

The monastery, under whose ancient shadow
Sits a silent monk

Prayers, faint like distant thunders
Small sins gathering, like rain in the valley

A row of sparrows settles on the eaves
Like a soul after another soul waiting to be delivered

And sunlight pierces into the grand hall
In an instant, dust cements into large pillars

At dusk, I finally see the thick canopy of a gingko
Under a rain cloud about to break

遗址

因为石柱已沉入海底
大殿的栋梁就只能生长在古老的森林里
同样，装饰花纹
还在缠绕枝头的藤蔓间

残存的石阶
证明了几何学比之精神
有更多的耐性
一只流浪狗独自坐着，如同
来自智利的考古学家

是废墟？也可以
是未完成的城堡，我也可能
只是提前到来

所有私人的造访
被挡在石砌坡道之外
我不代表世界
但我知道，它的存在已被什么人允许

一代代的小吏
渔夫、投机商……
曾从四面八方赶来，在山脚下
建造集镇、城市
在海洋和沉默的宫殿间穿梭

The Ruins

As the stone pillars have sunk to the bottom of the sea
The beams of the grand hall must grow in the ancient forest
Likewise, twines still wind their decorative patterns
Over the branches

The remaining stone steps testify
Geometry, which is more resilient
Than human spirit
A stray dog sits alone
Like an archeologist from Chile

Are these the ruins
Or an unfinished castle
Perhaps I have arrived too early

Every private visit is banned
From the cobble ramps
I do not represent the world, but I know
Someone has allowed its existence

Generations of petty officials
Fishermen, opportunistic investors, and so forth
Arrived from all corners and built towns and cities
At the foot of the mountain range, crisscrossing
Between the sea and the silent palace

现在，夜晚来临
街道已拥有了新的名字，门廊下的异国妇人
仍保留着
古老壁画中美丽的侧影，伴随着

无数次地震和雷电
无数次死于战争、宫庭谋杀以及
神秘的诅咒

详尽的资料，带我们
穿过黑暗的世纪和摇曳烛光
但没有提及
园林中失传的神秘的嬉戏……

这里的居民冷漠
但海洋无私，每天都从海底
掏出贝壳、死鱼，还有无穷无尽的
泡沫

Now it is night
The streets have new names, on the patio
Foreign ladies maintain their fine silhouettes
From ancient frescos, along with

Countless earthquakes and thunders
Countless deaths in wars, murders in court
And mysterious curses

Ample materials take us through
The dark century and the rocking lamp
Yet they do not mention
The lost, mystifying frolics in the gardens . . .

The inhabitants here are indifferent
But the sea is selfless, every day from whose bottom
Shells, dead fish, and endless foams are pulled out
And pooled

隐秘

我们住进一座老建筑
改建的旅馆，并不知道它的过去
穿堂风仍旧按时
从房子深处吹来，仿佛一些不死的灵魂
瘫躺在过道上的狗，没有吠叫
或许，它已辩认出我们其中的一个
一扇木门后面并未掩藏什么
“那么是谁移走了
我们发现真相和历史的权力”
一阵嬉笑后，我们看到
暗中还坐着一个男人
他脸上的平静
像这傍晚时突然中止的思考
我想到，这张脸的后面可能
曾有过另一张沮丧的脸。当他转过来
看着有人举着灯，手里拿着
刀、绳索和毒药进来
然后，雾霭和一阵淡淡的迷香涌入
请不必悲伤，阳光依然会照进小木窗
不久以后，鸡冠花仍将在身后
荒芜的地方盛放，因为
那里本来就是草木的世界

The Obscurity

Not knowing its past, we check into the hotel
That was converted from an old building
The wind through the courtyard still passes on time
Like undying souls from the depth of the house
The dog in the hallway, lying on its back
Does not bark, perhaps it recognizes one of us
Nothing is hidden behind the wooden door
Someone says, who has then removed our right
To discover history and truth
After a laugh, we see a man
Sitting in the dark
And the calm on his face
As if thoughts cut short at the twilight hour
It comes to me there must have been another
Dispirited face behind this one, when he turns around
And sees someone coming in with a lamp
Who is holding a sword, ropes, and poison
And then a fog and a fine scent permeate the air, there's no need
To sulk, sunlight still shines through the little wooden window
And soon after, the cockscombs are going to bloom
In a bleak place behind us, because there reigns
The world of grasses and trees

在展厅

两个中年男人，在一张古代地图前
寻找自己身处的位置

青铜鸟，已经腐烂
更像贾科梅蒂

铜镜似乎永远只展示
背面的花纹，因为对着它的脸已经消逝

几个教授模样的人
正在小声争论，一束射灯的光
照在他们头上

事实上，很多知识分子
用大量时间来钻研历史

但雷电、火
咳嗽和冻住的毛笔
都是难以忍受的

或许，他们只是喜欢部分
如花园、酒、绸缎和尽可能多的
侍女，安静、无声

像这一尊石像
她低垂着头，面容被内心专注的

In the Exhibition Hall

Two middle-aged men before an ancient map
Look for where they are

The bronze birds are now rotten
Closer to Giacometti

The bronze mirror seems forever to show nothing
But patterns on its back because the face that faces it is gone

A few professor types are having a discussion
In a low voice, a beam of spotlight
Shines on their heads

In fact, many intellectuals spend much time
Researching history

Yet thunder, lightning, fire
Coughs and frozen brushes
Remain all too unbearable

Perhaps they just like parts of it
Such as silk, wine, garden, or as many
A maid as possible, quiet, soundless

Like this stone statue
Head hanging low, her face locked

微笑锁住

发髻、鼻，微妙的嘴角
都非常生动，不像雕刻

更像是有一只手
拂去了原先深埋在她脸上的尘灰

而灰尘漂浮
在通向外面街道的走廊上

那里戴鸭舌帽的
新一代摄影师，试图捕捉
这座城市的生活气息

旁边，一条古老的河流里
生成出阵阵薄雾

In an attentively absorbing smile

Delicate mouth, nose, hairdo
So vivid, unlikely sculpted

More like a hand
Had brushed off the dust buried deep in her face

And the dust floats
In the hallway that leads to the street

There is a new-generation photographer
Wearing a cap, who tries to capture
The breath and beat of this city

By his side, an ancient river boils
Bursts of thin mist

谬误

蛇的谬误在于没有水它却在游动

蝙蝠的困境是总会面对
两个可供选择的世界，因此它倒挂像一笔欠账

这期间，一只苹果落地

为什么短暂的人类
有如此多含混不清的历史，像黎明时分的困倦
重重地压在眼睑上

而上天昏聩，总是忘了从箱柜里摸出的是什么
一会儿是瘟疫和杀戮
一会儿是鲜花和海浪

The Fallacy

The fallacy of the snake is that it wiggles without water

The difficulty of the bat is that it faces two worlds
To choose from, so it hangs upside down like debt

Meanwhile, an apple lands in its swirl

Why does the short-lived mankind possess
So many ambiguous histories, like the drowsiness at dawn
That weighs heavily on the eyelids

The amnesiac gods always forget what's fished out from the trunk
For a moment, pandemics and slaughters
For another, fresh flowers and oceanic waves

候车室

凌晨时分，候车室
深邃的大厅像一种睡意

在我身边，很多人
突然起身离开，仿佛一群隐匿的
听到密令的圣徒

有人打电话，有人系鞋带
有人说再见（也许不再）

那些不允许带走的
物件和狗
被小四轮车无声推走

生活就是一个幻觉
一位年长的诗人告诉我
（他刚刚在瞌睡中醒来）

就如同你在雨水冰冷的站台上
手里拎着越来越重的
总感觉是别人的一个包裹

The Waiting Room

At the blue hour, the depthless hall
Of the waiting room falls into somnolence

By my side, many people take leave
Out of the blue, like a group of hidden saints
Who have just received secret orders

Someone is on the phone, someone ties his shoes
Someone says goodbye (or no more)

Those items and dogs
That may not be taken away are now pushed
Quietly by a little flatbed quadricycle

Life is an illusion
An older poet tells me
(He just woke from a nap)

As if on a cold and rainy platform
You carry a heavier and heavier bag
And always feel it belongs to someone else

蚕丝

它令我想到
某个早晨旧上海弄堂
窗口外的阵阵白雾

或者是，大革命前
江浙一带，被缠绕着的
晦暗不明的灵魂

The Silk

It reminds me
Of a morning in an old alley in Shanghai
Bursts of white fog outside the window

Or before the great revolution
In the Yangtze Delta, the obscure
Souls, entwined

幸福总是在傍晚到来

幸福总是在
傍晚到来，而阴影靠得太近

我记起一座小城
五月的气息突然充斥在人行道和
藤蔓低垂的拱门

在我的身体中
酿造一种致幻的蜜

脸从陌生街道的
深处一一浮出，一如询问：你为何
站在这里？我不记得

我只知道
那无数丢失的白天、窗口突然关闭
名字在末尾淡去
如同烟雾

我走在街上，一滴雨水
落在额上，这又喻示着什么
觉醒可能要等到夜晚

也许，不会太晚
一座寺院
终于在默祷中拥有了寂静

Happiness Always Comes at Twilight

Happiness always comes
At twilight, and shadows lean too close

I remember a small town
The smell of May immediately fills the sidewalk
And the arch drips with tendrils

Inside my body
Hypnotic honey is being made

Faces from the deep
Of strange streets surface one by one as if asking: why
Are you standing here? I do not remember

I only know the countless days lost
The windows, suddenly closed
Names fade toward their own end
Like smoke

I walk on the street, a drop of rain falls
On my forehead, what does this say
Wait perhaps until evening to awake

Perhaps not too late
A temple finally attains
Its calm in silent prayers

在它的外面
几只羊正在吃草，缓慢地
如同黑暗吃掉光线

Outside it
A few sheep graze grass, so slowly
As if darkness eats away light

野鸭与白鹭

野鸭和白鹭
停在离岸不远的湖中
头朝向浅岸,石头还有芦苇
一棵乌桕微微晃动,几个小时
野鸭在睡，穿着那件
老旧的蓑衣，白鹭注视着它
或轻灵地收起一只脚，佯装俯瞰
水草摇曳，天空湛蓝
像在某种远古的时间里
白鹭和野鸭，它们之间的静谧
隔着白光和灰暗的倒影
隔着不同的时代
突然野鸭飞走了，傲慢的嘴
肥硕的尾，从湖面上升起
只留下白鹭，独自站在一片涟漪里
湖面之上是正午酷热的寂静

The Mallard and the Egret

The mallard and the egret
Stop at the lake not far from the shoreline
And look toward the shallow bank, rocks, and reeds
A Chinese tallow shakes lightly, for hours
The mallard sleeps, wearing its old
Straw coat, the egret stares at it or swiftly
Tucks in a foot, faking for a bird's-eye view
Over swishing water grasses, the sky translucent
Blue as if in an ancient age
The egret and the mallard, between them the serenity
Set apart by daylight and pale shadows
Set apart by different spheres of time
The mallard suddenly flies away, its arrogant beak
And fat tail rising from the lake, leaving the egret
That stands alone in a realm of ripples
Above the lake, the midday burns into stillness

大地

古云杉能成活上万年
蚂蚁懂得如何
避开胡椒，在古代
你不会看到番茄，但这些看起来
就是现在它们共处的大地
也曾是恐龙和桫椤的大地
在它之上，巨型鸟已经绝迹
只有无数条闪着光的航线
在穿行，无人机如飞蛾
追随着一列神秘的列车遁入
峡谷的黑夜。一个孕妇
起身喝水如满月，江河将被驯服
不远处的监狱里，惯犯
已在上铺熟睡，鼾声听上去
有如《命运》的前奏

The Earth

An ancient spruce lives up to ten thousand years
An ant knows how
To avoid peppers, in antiquity
You wouldn't see a tomato, yet the earth
That seems to coexist with all these today was also
The earth for dinosaurs and flying spider-monkey ferns
The giant birds have died out
Only countless flickering lines of flight
Keep crossing, and like a moth, a drone
Follows a mysterious train and falls
Into the valley of night, a pregnant lady rises
To drink like a full moon, rivers will be tamed
In a nearby prison, a regular inmate
Sleeps soundly on the upper bunk, snoring
Like the prelude to the *Symphony of Fate*

高速公路

高速公路
像一种幻象，在粗陋的地面
隔离了两边破败的
村镇、人群

犹如一根黑亮的绸带

有一天，我们的灵魂
是否也可以这样离开，沿着这条
深不见底的河流
永无尽头

The Highway

The highway looks
Like an illusion, on the pitted ground
Separating on both sides
Decaying towns and crowds

Like a bright and black ribbon

One day, can our souls
Leave like this, along this
Bottomless river
Endlessly

注视

很多昆虫
只生活在暗影里，薄荷
只要小剂量的光
在古老的院子里，现在和
记忆并不轮值，空气中
青草的气息，其实是
收割的气息。有一扇窗子
会打开，镂空雕喜欢的阴影
会使石狮子复活：毛发疯长
利爪蜷缩，它的安静只是
一种屏息，犹如谈判中的对峙
中间会有人离开，去洗手间打电话
旁边，眼窝深陷的女人
目空一切（只喜欢吊坠）
夜晚很快来临，夜里全是黑的，没有倒影
只有楼梯道里昏暗的
交易在进行。美术馆里
有一盏射灯，仿佛永远照着一张画
（它被盯死了）。老鼠在下水道
进进出出，仿佛在看天有没有亮
晨曦首先出现在树冠上
里面藏着几只寻常的鸟。而中午
诗人会坐在树荫下
注视着明亮的广场，因为
在强光下你会看不清轮廓

The Gaze

Many insects
Only live in the dark, mints
Need just a small dose of light
In an ancient courtyard, the present and memories
Do not take turns to keep watch, in the air
The smell of grass is in fact
The smell of harvest, a window opens
Letting in the shadows preferred by hollow carving
To bring a stone lion back to life: hair wildly growing
Sharp claws curled, whose stillness holds
Its breath, like a confrontation in a negotiation
During which someone may leave to make a call in the bathroom
While a nearby lady with sunken eyes looks down
On the world (she likes nothing but jewelry)
Night quickly arrives, all black, no reflection
But dingy transactions on the stairway
Are taking place, in the art museum
A spotlight seems to always shine on one painting
(As if deadly fixed), a rat in the gutter
Runs in and out, as if to see whether it is day again
Dawn appears first on a canopy
Where a few ordinary birds hide, at midday
A poet sits in the shade of a tree
Staring at the lit square, as you cannot make out
Any contours in the dazzling light

流星事件

没有秘密的人
会受到最严厉的审讯

靠近他，排列着
所知甚少的白痴、失忆者，丧偶的人

几棵不育的石榴夹杂其中
老人、白头翁、杨树瑟瑟发抖的鞭子

我靠后。我有一些小罪，包括一些
寺院外听到的东西

三个鸡奸犯，站在我后面
他们是审判官的妹夫和堂亲

聪明的群山沉默着
流星，又一次落到了邻村

The Meteor Event

A person without secrets
Bears the most severe trial

Ignorant idiots, amnesiacs, widowers
Lining up by his side

The elderly, Chinese bulbuls, poplars' shaking whips
And a couple sterile pomegranates in the mix

I step back, I have a few petty crimes, including
A number of things overheard outside the monastery

Three sodomites stand behind me
They are the brothers-in-law and cousins of the judge

The sly mountain range shuts its mouth
Meteors, once again, fall onto the neighboring village

墓地

从村上看
墓地，安静灰暗
像前朝

只有刺莓艳丽
仿佛死去的嫔妃

旋风裹着黄叶
一段崩塌的
岁月，在楝树下

有越来越
深沉的恐惧，史官
虚弱，半躺着

一只乌鸦
停在枝头，它不知道
即使终其一生
棺木也不会打开，

命运
不会被揭示

而夜里
白色蔷薇依然开放
被一束冷淡的光
永远照亮

The Graveyard

Seen from the village
The graveyard, quiet and gray
Looks like a past dynasty

Only the Christ thorn dazzles
Like dead concubines

A whirlwind wrapped in yellow leaves
A period of days and nights
Collapsed, under the bead tree

A terror grows
Deeper and deeper, a historian
Ailing, half lying

A crow
Stops on the branch, it doesn't know
Even with a whole life
The casket will not open

Fate will not
Be revealed

And at night
White roses bloom as usual
Forever illuminated
By a ray of indifferent light

房子

1

房子不能建立在
蛇蝎之地。狗不能与人争食

要警惕门楣
不要轻易踏入倒屋，尽管
倾塌自有其命运

The House

1

A house mustn't be built in a land of scorpions and snakes
A dog and a man mustn't compete for food

Be alert of the lintel
Don't simply enter a fallen abode, although
A collapse has its own fate

2

在三角形的院落
有时你能看到令人窒息的身影

但如果桃花
不在其位开放，灾难就会如同
一颗流星

2

In a triangular courtyard
Sometimes you may see breathtaking figures

But when peach blossoms
Bloom in the wrong place, a catastrophe
Then shoots like a meteor

3

在西墙上撒尿
不能在灶膛边做爱

倘若乞丐
在土地庙里动土，秀才就会
失足于沟渠

3

Piss on the west wall
Don't make love by the stove

If a beggar moves dirt
In a village temple, a scholar
Then steps into a ditch

4

井水不能清洗屋面
房子与房子间隔着一道永恒的深渊

在夜里，它们高大冷酷
仿佛穿着黑袍的圣徒，肃默排列着
等待召唤

4

Water from the well mustn't be used to wash the roof
An eternal abyss separates one house from another

At night, they are cold and tall
Like saints in black robes, somberly arrayed
For the beckoning

女巫

在桥上
村上的一个女巫
告诉我

你什么也
看不清，因为你们的眼里
有世世代代的迷雾

The Witch

On the bridge
A village witch
Tells me

You see nothing
Clearly, since in all your eyes
A fog gathers generations

Acknowledgments

Gratitude to a grant from the PEN/Heim Translation Fund. Sincere thanks to the whole team at Deep Vellum, especially Shook for their generous editorial guidance.

Many thanks to the editors and readers of the magazines in which these translations or their earlier versions first appeared:

128 Lit: The Moon, The Puppet Metaphor
The Arkansas International: The Laughter, Shanghai at Night, In the Dark, Elsewhere, The Dog-Eared Book
Asymptote: The Fireflies, At the Candy Shop, In the Countryside, The Uncanny Town
Bennington Review: A Poem on the Chinese Perspective on Fate
Blackbird: The Mallard and the Egret, The Gaze, The Silk
The Cincinnati Review: The Ruins, The Stranger
Circumference: The Soul, The Season When Fruit Trees Sprout and Bloom, The Correspondence
Copihue Poetry: The Prophecy, The Highspeed Train, The Obscurity
Guernica: The Waiting Room
The Kenyon Review: The Long View
Lana Turner: The Fallacy, The Meteor Event, Happiness Always Comes at Twilight
The Massachusetts Review: In the Exhibition Hall, The Highway
Nashville Review: The Graveyard
Poetry: The Witch, The Connection
Poetry Daily: The Gaze (reprint)

Poetry Northwest: The Earth
Zócalo Public Square: The High-Flying Birds

Nominated for *Best Literary Translations* anthology 2024–2025: The Moon, The Puppet Metaphor
Nominated for *Best Literary Translations* anthology 2025–2026: The Mallard and the Egret, The Gaze, The Silk, The Ruins, The Stranger
Longlisted for *Best Literary Translations* anthology 2025–2026: The Stranger

YE Hui is an acclaimed Chinese metaphysical poet who lives in Nanjing. He is the author of three poetry collections, 《在糖果店》(*At the Candy Shop*; Hungyeh Publishing, 1999), 《对应》(*The Correspondence*; Flower City Publishing House, 2009), and 《遗址》(*The Ruins*; Shanghai EP/Changjiang Literature & Art Publishing House, 2019). His poems in English translation have appeared or are forthcoming in *128 Lit, The Arkansas International, Asymptote, Bennington Review, Blackbird, Cincinnati Review, Circumference, Copihue Poetry, Guernica, The Kenyon Review, Lana Turner, The Massachusetts Review, Nashville Review, Poetry, Poetry Northwest,* and *Zocálo Public Square.* The English full-length translation of his latest collection, *The Ruins*, was awarded a PEN/Heim Translation Fund Grant.

Dong LI is a multilingual author who translates from Chinese, English, French, and German. He is the English translator of the PEN/Heim-winning *The Gleaner Song* (Giramondo/Deep Vellum, 2021) by the Chinese poet SONG Lin, and *The Wild Great Wall* (Deep Vellum, 2018) by the Chinese poet ZHU Zhu. His debut collection of poetry *The Orange Tree* (University of Chicago Press, 2023) was the inaugural winner of the Phoenix Emerging Poet Book Prize and a finalist for the Poetry Society of America's Four Quartets Prize.

www.ingramcontent.com/pod-product-compliance
Lightning Source LLC
Jackson TN
JSHW080715071025
91577JS00002B/1

9781646054053